JAY GERMAN

Real Estate Investing Hacks

How to Start a Thriving Real Estate Business While Working Full Time

This book was professionally typeset on Reedsy.
Find out more at reedsy.com

Contents

1

Introduction

Welcome to your essential guide for navigating the world of real estate investment alongside a full-time job. This book is crafted for individuals short on time but eager to step into real estate investing, aiming to provide a straightforward, step-by-step blueprint to success without sacrificing your current professional commitments.

The core message here is clear: embarking on a real estate investment journey doesn't require giving up your day job. Instead, it demands smart planning, strategic time management, and the cultivation of key relationships. This guide stands out by offering practical, actionable advice, breaking down the process into manageable steps that fit into your busy schedule.

The motivation behind this book is to debunk the myth that real estate investing is off-limits to those with full-time jobs. With the right approach, anyone can build a successful real estate portfolio. This book will show you how to use your limited time wisely, ensuring each action you take moves you closer to your investment goals.

We start with the importance of building relationships in the real estate sector. It's not just about who you know; it's about who knows you and the value you bring to the table. We'll cover how to integrate yourself into the real estate community, gaining access to deals and opportunities that aren't available to the general public.

Identifying your "North Star" is next, helping you set clear, achievable goals. This clarity is crucial for navigating the complexities of real estate investing. Following that, we'll explore methods to enhance your productivity, ensuring you make the most out of every hour dedicated to your real estate ventures.

Accountability is a key theme, with strategies to keep you on track toward your investment objectives. The chapter on winning focuses on leveraging initial successes for future gains, emphasizing the importance of momentum in building a prosperous real estate business.

This book is direct and to the point, providing the essential knowledge needed to succeed in real estate investing while maintaining a full-time job. It's designed for immediate application, suitable for beginners and seasoned investors alike.

As we move forward, remember that success in real estate investing comes from informed decisions, perseverance, and a clear focus on your goals. Your full-time job can complement, rather than hinder, your investment aspirations.

This introduction sets the stage for a journey of discovery and achievement in real estate investing. Through focused, practical advice, you're about to learn how to build a thriving real estate business, quickly generating income and laying the groundwork for long-term wealth.

Let's get started.

2

Establish Relationships

I n real estate investing, your network is your net worth. This chapter delves into the foundational step of establishing relationships within the real estate sector, specifically focusing on leveraging local real estate investing associations and networking with other investors. The goal is to cultivate a network that not only supports your growth in the industry but also opens doors to opportunities that would otherwise remain out of reach.

Find a Local Real Estate Investing Association

Embarking on your real estate investment journey begins with surrounding yourself with like-minded individuals who share your ambition and passion. A local real estate investing association (REIA) serves as an excellent starting point. These associations are not just clubs; they are incubators for growth, learning, and opportunity in the real estate domain. By joining a REIA, you place yourself in an environment ripe with knowledge, experience, and the potential for partnerships.

Benefits of Joining a REIA:

- **Education:** REIAs frequently host speakers, workshops, and seminars on a variety of topics relevant to real estate investing. From market trends and legal aspects to financing options and property management, these sessions provide a wealth of information that can save you both time and money.
- **Networking:** The core of REIAs is the opportunity to meet and connect with other investors. These relationships can lead to joint ventures, partnerships, and access to deals that you might not find through traditional channels.
- **Resources:** Many REIAs offer resources such as contract templates, investment tools, and access to discounted services. These can be invaluable, especially when you're starting out.
- **Support:** Real estate investing can be a complex and sometimes daunting endeavor. Being part of a REIA gives you access to a community of peers and mentors who can offer advice, share their experiences, and provide moral support.
- **Market Insights:** Understanding your local market is crucial in real estate investing. REIAs offer insights into local market conditions, investment strategies that are working, and upcoming areas for investment.

Finding Your Local REIA:

To locate a REIA near you, start with a simple online search using keywords like "real estate investing association" + your city or region. Websites like National Real Estate Investors Association (NationalREIA.org) provide directories of local associations. Social media platforms and real estate forums can also be excellent resources for finding local groups.

Once you've identified a REIA, take the next step by attending a meeting or event. Approach this with an open mind and a readiness to learn and engage. Remember, the value you get from joining a REIA is proportional to the effort and enthusiasm you bring to the table.

Joining a REIA is a strategic move for anyone serious about building a successful real estate investment business. It's about more than just attending meetings; it's about actively participating in a community that can propel you towards your investment goals.

Seek Out Opportunities or Relationships Where You Can Provide Value

In the realm of real estate investing, building a network is not just about collecting contacts; it's about establishing meaningful relationships where mutual value can be exchanged. As you engage with your local real estate investing association and meet other investors, focus on how you can contribute to these relationships as much as, if not more than, what you can gain from them.

Benefits of Providing Value:

- **Reputation Building:** Consistently offering help, sharing knowledge, or connecting people within your network enhances your reputation as a valuable and generous member of the community. This reputation can open doors to opportunities and deals.
- **Reciprocity:** The principle of reciprocity is powerful; when you help others, they are more inclined to help you in return. Whether it's finding deals, securing financing, or navigating challenges, the support you've given often comes back to assist you when you need it.

- **Learning Through Teaching:** Sharing your knowledge with others reinforces your own understanding and often leads to new insights as you articulate concepts or solve problems together.
- **Expanding Your Network:** By being a source of value, you'll find that your network expands organically. People are more likely to introduce you to their contacts, significantly broadening your circle of potential partners, mentors, and friends.

How to Provide Value:

- **Share Insights:** If you come across valuable market data, share it with your network. Being seen as a source of timely and relevant information can make you a go-to person within your investment community.
- **Leverage Your Skills:** Offer your unique skills or expertise to others. Whether it's financial analysis, marketing, or legal knowledge, your skills can be invaluable to someone just starting out or looking to expand their business.
- **Connect People:** Act as a connector within your network. Introducing people who can benefit from each other's services or partnerships fosters a sense of community and collaboration.

Providing value within your real estate network is about fostering a culture of support and generosity. This approach not only enriches your professional relationships but also sets a strong foundation for your own success in the real estate investing world.

Closing Thoughts:

Establishing strong relationships within the real estate community is a critical step in building a successful investment business. It requires effort, consistency, and a genuine interest in contributing to the success of others. By following these steps, you'll not only expand your network but also position yourself as a credible and valued member of the local real estate investing community. Remember, the strength of your relationships often determines the height of your success in real estate investing.

3

Get Inside the Real Estate Circle

E ntering the inner circle of the real estate business is a strategic move that can significantly accelerate your journey as an investor. One of the most effective ways to achieve this is by obtaining your real estate salesperson license. This step is not just about facilitating transactions; it's about immersing yourself in the industry, gaining access to valuable information, and connecting with key players in the field.

Benefits of Getting Your Real Estate License

Obtaining your real estate salesperson license as a new investor is a strategic move that opens up a multitude of benefits, significantly enhancing your capability to succeed in the real estate market. Here's how:

- **Direct Access to the MLS:** Having your license grants you direct access to the Multiple Listing Service (MLS), a comprehensive database of current property listings. This access is invaluable for conducting detailed market research, understanding pricing trends, and identifying potential investment opportunities as soon as they hit the market.

- **Increased Earning Potential:** With a real estate license, you can earn commissions by representing clients in buying and selling properties. This additional income stream can be significant and can be reinvested into your own real estate ventures, providing the financial flexibility to grow your investment portfolio.
- **Enhanced Credibility:** Being a licensed real estate agent adds a layer of credibility to your investment business. Clients, partners, and other stakeholders tend to trust licensed professionals more, which can be a considerable advantage in negotiations and when forming new business relationships.
- **Educational Opportunities:** The process of obtaining your license involves comprehensive study that covers various aspects of real estate transactions, laws, ethics, and property management. This education equips you with a deeper understanding of the market, enabling you to make more informed investment decisions.
- **Network Expansion:** Real estate is a relationship-driven business. As a licensed agent, you'll naturally meet a wide array of industry professionals, including other agents, brokers, lenders, and investors. Each of these connections can offer new opportunities, insights, and partnerships that are invaluable for a growing investor.
- **Insight into the Industry:** Working as a real estate agent provides a unique perspective on the industry, offering insights into buyer and seller behaviors, market dynamics, and effective marketing strategies. This knowledge can be directly applied to your investment strategies, giving you a competitive edge.

By obtaining a real estate salesperson license, you not only diversify your income but also deepen your market knowledge, enhance your professional network, and increase your overall effectiveness as a real estate investor.

Exposure to Off-Market or In-Office Listings

One of the most compelling reasons for a new investor to obtain a real estate license is the access it provides to off-market or in-office listings. These are properties that are not listed on the public MLS or are available exclusively through broker networks. The benefits of tapping into this hidden market are significant:

- **First-Mover Advantage:** Off-market listings are less exposed to the competitive pressures of the open market, giving you the opportunity to negotiate deals without the frenzy of multiple offers that is common with publicly listed properties.
- **Better Deals:** Properties that are sold off-market often go for prices that are closer to the seller's true bottom line, as there's less competition driving the price up. This can result in better deals and higher potential profits for your investment.
- **Exclusive Access:** Having a real estate license often means you're part of a brokerage or agent network that shares these exclusive listings. This insider access can be a goldmine for finding unique investment opportunities that are invisible to the general investing public.
- **Stronger Relationships:** Working directly with other realtors and brokers on off-market deals helps build strong professional relationships. These connections can be incredibly beneficial over time, as they may think of you first when new opportunities arise.
- **Negotiation Leverage:** Being in the know about off-market listings and having direct relationships with listing agents can give you more leverage in negotiations. You'll have a better understanding of the seller's situation and can tailor your offer accordingly.

- **Portfolio Diversity:** Off-market and in-office listings can introduce you to a wider variety of property types and investment opportunities, helping you build a more diversified real estate portfolio.

Leveraging your status as a licensed real estate professional to gain access to off-market and in-office listings can dramatically enhance your investment strategy, providing opportunities for growth and profitability that are not available through traditional channels.

Property Valuation

Mastering property valuation is a cornerstone of successful real estate investing. As a licensed real estate professional, you gain access to tools, resources, and insights that enable you to accurately determine the value of potential investment properties. Understanding how to properly assess property value is crucial for several reasons:

- **Informed Decision Making:** Accurate property valuation ensures that you make informed investment decisions. By understanding the true market value of a property, you can determine whether an investment aligns with your financial goals and risk tolerance.
- **Identifying Opportunities:** Being adept at property valuation helps you quickly identify opportunities that others might overlook. You can spot underpriced properties that offer high potential returns, as well as avoid overpriced listings that could lead to financial underperformance.
- **Negotiation Power:** Knowledge of a property's value strengthens your position in negotiations. You can confidently argue your offer price based on solid market data, making it more likely that you'll secure properties at favorable terms.
- **Investment Analysis:** Proper valuation is essential for conducting

thorough investment analysis. It allows you to calculate key financial metrics, such as the return on investment (ROI), cap rate, and cash flow projections, with greater accuracy. This analysis is vital for comparing different investment opportunities and selecting the best ones.

- **Financing and Appraisal:** Lenders often require appraisals to determine a property's value for financing purposes. Understanding how properties are valued can help you anticipate how lenders will view the deal, potentially smoothing the path to securing financing.

- **Risk Management:** By accurately valuing properties, you can better assess and manage the risks associated with real estate investment. Knowing the market value helps you set appropriate rent prices, estimate potential profits, and make contingency plans for market fluctuations.

- **Market Trends Awareness:** The process of property valuation involves analyzing current market trends, including supply and demand dynamics, recent sales data, and economic indicators. This awareness can inform your broader investment strategy, helping you to time your investments wisely.

Gaining proficiency in property valuation not only enhances your ability to make smarter investment choices but also elevates your overall understanding of the real estate market. As a licensed real estate professional, leveraging this skill can lead to more successful investment outcomes, positioning you for long-term growth and profitability in the real estate sector.

How to Obtain Your Real Estate Salesperson License

Embarking on the journey to become a licensed real estate salesperson is a pivotal step towards deepening your involvement in the real estate market. The process to obtain your license is structured but varies by state, reflecting local laws and requirements. Here's a comprehensive guide to navigating this path:

- **Understand Your State's Requirements:** The first step is to familiarize yourself with the specific requirements of your state. These can typically be found on the website of your state's real estate commission or department of real estate. Requirements usually include a minimum age, educational prerequisites, a background check, and passing a licensing examination.
- **Enroll in Pre-Licensing Courses:** Almost every state mandates a set number of hours of pre-licensing education, which can be completed at accredited real estate schools or, in some cases, online. These courses cover essential topics such as real estate principles, law, ethics, contracts, and property management. The aim is to prepare you comprehensively for the state exam and your future career in real estate.
- **Choose the Right Education Provider:** Selecting a reputable education provider is crucial. Look for schools or online platforms that offer courses approved by your state's real estate commission and have a high pass rate for their students on the state exam. Some providers also offer exam prep courses, which can be invaluable in ensuring your success.
- **Pass Your State's Licensing Exam:** After completing your pre-licensing education, you'll need to pass your state's real estate licensing exam. This exam typically covers national real estate principles and laws, as well as state-specific laws. The exam is

14

divided into sections, and you must achieve a passing score in each section. Preparing thoroughly for this exam is key, as it tests both your knowledge of real estate fundamentals and your understanding of state-specific regulations.

· **Select a Sponsoring Broker:** Before you can practice as a real estate agent, you'll need to be sponsored by a licensed real estate broker. This broker will act as your mentor and provide you with the guidance needed to navigate your early career. When selecting a sponsoring broker, consider factors such as the broker's reputation, training opportunities, commission structure, and whether their business model aligns with your career goals.

· **Complete the Application Process:** Once you've passed the licensing exam and chosen a sponsoring broker, you can complete your application for a real estate license. This process includes submitting your proof of completed education, exam results, application forms, and any other documentation required by your state. There will also be a fee associated with the application.

· **Background Check and Fingerprinting:** As part of the application process, most states require a background check and fingerprinting to ensure the integrity of its real estate professionals. This step is standard and helps maintain high ethical standards within the industry.

· **Engage in Continuous Education:** After obtaining your license, remember that learning and development in the real estate field are ongoing. Most states require real estate professionals to complete continuing education (CE) courses to renew their licenses regularly. These courses ensure that you stay up-to-date with the latest industry practices, laws, and ethical standards.

Closing Thoughts:

Obtaining your real estate salesperson license is a proactive step toward becoming a central figure in your local real estate market. It opens up a new realm of possibilities for income, networking, and investment opportunities. By aligning your credential as a real estate agent with your investment goals, you position yourself to recognize and capitalize on opportunities that others might miss. This dual approach not only accelerates your path to success in real estate investing but also deepens your understanding and expertise in the industry.

4

What is Your North Star?

I dentifying your North Star in real estate investing is about pinpointing the guiding principle that directs all your investment decisions. This chapter delves into determining your investment strategy and building goals around it to ensure sustained progress over time. Understanding your investment strategy is akin to choosing your path in the vast realm of real estate. Whether it's fix and flip, buy and hold, short-term rental, tax default investing, wholetail, creative finance, or note investing, each strategy comes with its own set of challenges and rewards. Your North Star is not just about what you do, but why you do it, guiding you through the complexities of the market and helping you stay focused on your long-term objectives.

Determine Your Investment Strategy

Fix and Flip

Fix and flip investing involves purchasing properties at a lower market value, renovating them, and then selling them at a profit. This strategy appeals to investors looking for short-term gains and who have an interest in real estate development and renovation. Here are the pros and cons of fix and flip investing, along with resources for further education.

Pros:

- **Quick Returns:** Fix and flip can yield significant profits in a relatively short amount of time, often within a few months to a year after purchase.
- **Tangible Improvements:** Investors have direct control over the renovations and improvements that can increase the property's value.
- **Market Flexibility:** Skilled flippers can profit in both rising and falling markets by purchasing undervalued properties and adding value through renovations.
- **Learning Opportunity:** Each project offers a chance to gain valuable experience in real estate, renovation, and market analysis.

Cons:

- **Capital Intensive:** Initial investments can be high, as purchasing and renovating properties requires significant upfront capital.
- **Risk of Loss:** There are risks involved, including unexpected renovation costs, longer than anticipated sale times, and market downturns, all of which can erode profits.
- **Time and Effort:** Fix and flip projects demand a considerable amount of time and effort, from managing renovations to handling sales, which can be challenging for those with other full-time commitments.
- **Market Knowledge:** Success requires a deep understanding of the local real estate market to accurately assess property values and renovation potentials.

Resources for Learning More:

- **Real Estate Investment Associations (REIAs):** Joining a local REIA can connect you with experienced flippers and educational workshops.
- **Online Courses and Webinars:** Platforms like Udemy, Coursera, and BiggerPockets offer courses on fix and flip strategies, financing, and project management.
- **Books:** Titles like "The Book on Flipping Houses" by J Scott provide comprehensive guides to all aspects of fix and flip investing.
- **Real Estate Investing Podcasts and Blogs:** Listening to podcasts and reading blogs from successful real estate investors can offer insights and tips tailored to the fix and flip market.
- **Networking Events:** Attending real estate networking events and seminars can provide opportunities to meet mentors and partners who have experience in fix and flip projects.

In conclusion, fix and flip investing can be highly profitable for those willing to put in the work and take on the risks. It requires a combination of market knowledge, renovation skills, and project management abilities. By leveraging the available resources for education and networking, investors can significantly increase their chances of success in the fix and flip market.

Buy and Hold

Buy and hold investing is a long-term strategy that involves purchasing real estate with the intention of renting it out to generate steady income and benefiting from appreciation over time. This approach is favored by investors looking for passive income streams and long-term capital growth. Here are the advantages and disadvantages of buy and hold investing, along with resources for further learning.

Pros:

- **Passive Income:** One of the biggest draws is the potential for generating consistent rental income, providing a steady cash flow that can cover the mortgage and operational costs, with surplus income as profit.
- **Long-Term Appreciation:** Over time, real estate typically appreciates in value, offering investors significant returns when they decide to sell, in addition to the income generated during the holding period.
- **Tax Benefits:** Buy and hold investors can take advantage of several tax deductions related to property ownership, including mortgage interest, property tax, operating expenses, depreciation, and repairs.
- **Inflation Hedge:** Real estate investments can act as a hedge against inflation, as property values and rents tend to increase with inflation, protecting the purchasing power of the investor's income.

Cons:

- **Liquidity:** Real estate is not a liquid asset, meaning it can take time to sell a property if cash is needed quickly.
- **Management Responsibilities:** Owning rental properties requires dealing with tenants, maintenance issues, and other management tasks, which can be time-consuming and stressful, although this can be mitigated by hiring a property management company.
- **Market Risks:** Real estate markets can fluctuate, and properties can decrease in value in the short term, affecting both rental income and the potential sale price.
- **Financial Commitment:** The initial financial outlay for purchasing

a property can be substantial, and investors must be prepared for ongoing costs, such as maintenance, insurance, and property taxes.

Resources for Learning More:

- **Real Estate Investment Associations (REIAs):** Membership can provide access to valuable networking opportunities, educational resources, and mentorship from experienced buy and hold investors.
- **Books:** Titles like "The Book on Rental Property Investing" by Brandon Turner offer in-depth guidance on building a successful buy and hold portfolio.
- **Online Platforms:** Websites such as BiggerPockets feature forums, articles, podcasts, and webinars dedicated to buy and hold investing, covering topics from property selection to financing and property management.
- **Educational Courses:** Online learning platforms like Udemy and Coursera offer courses specifically focused on buy and hold real estate strategies, property management, and financial analysis.
- **Networking Events and Seminars:** These can be invaluable for connecting with other investors, learning from their experiences, and finding potential investment opportunities.

Buy and hold investing offers a compelling mix of passive income, long-term wealth accumulation, and tax advantages. Despite its challenges, such as property management and market variability, the strategy remains a cornerstone of many successful real estate investment portfolios. By leveraging educational resources and connecting with the real estate community, investors can navigate the complexities of buy and hold investing and build a profitable and sustainable portfolio.

Short Term Rental

Short term rental investing involves renting out properties on a nightly, weekly, or monthly basis, typically facilitated by platforms such as Airbnb, VRBO, or Booking.com. This strategy caters to travelers and provides an alternative to traditional hotel accommodations, offering investors a way to capitalize on the growing demand for flexible lodging options. Here are the benefits and challenges of short term rental investing, along with resources for further education.

Pros:

- **Higher Potential Income:** Short term rentals can yield significantly higher returns than traditional long-term leases, as nightly rates are usually higher than monthly rent prices.
- **Market Flexibility:** Investors can adjust prices based on demand, season, and special events, optimizing earnings throughout the year.
- **Diversification:** Offering short term rentals can diversify an investment portfolio, spreading risk across different types of real estate investments.
- **Personal Use:** Owners have the flexibility to block out dates for personal use, enjoying the benefits of the property themselves.

Cons:

- **Regulatory Challenges:** Many cities have regulations that limit or restrict short term rentals, requiring permits or imposing taxes, which can impact profitability.
- **Higher Operational Costs:** Short term rentals incur higher maintenance, cleaning, and furnishing costs compared to long-term rentals.

- **Income Variability:** Income can be unpredictable, with seasonal fluctuations affecting occupancy rates and overall earnings.
- **Management Intensity:** Successful short term rentals require active management, including guest communication, cleaning, and repairs, demanding more time and effort from the investor.

Resources for Learning More:

- **Online Platforms:** Airbnb and VRBO offer host education resources, community forums, and market insights specific to short term rental operations.
- **Books:** "The Airbnb Way" by Joseph Michelli provides insights into creating outstanding guest experiences, while "Optimize YOUR Bnb" by Daniel Rusteen offers practical tips for maximizing rental income.
- **Podcasts and Blogs:** Listening to podcasts like "Get Paid for Your Pad" and reading blogs focused on short term rentals can offer current strategies, tips, and industry trends.
- **Courses and Webinars:** Websites such as Udemy and Skillshare offer courses on starting and managing short term rentals, covering topics from pricing strategies to guest communication.
- **Networking Groups:** Joining local or online real estate investment groups focused on short term rentals can provide valuable insights, support, and potential partnerships.

Short term rental investing offers a lucrative opportunity for those willing to navigate its complexities and invest the necessary time and resources into creating exceptional guest experiences. Despite the challenges, including regulatory hurdles and operational demands, the strategy can yield high returns and provide a flexible investment option in the dynamic real estate market. By utilizing the wealth of available educational resources and connecting with other investors, you can successfully tap into the short term rental market and grow your real estate investment portfolio.

Tax Default Investing

Tax default investing involves purchasing properties that are in default due to unpaid property taxes. Investors can acquire properties at a fraction of their market value through tax lien certificates or tax deed sales. This form of investment offers a unique avenue for entering the real estate market but comes with its own set of challenges and opportunities. Here's an overview of the pros and cons of tax default investing, along with resources for further education.

Pros:

- **High Return Potential:** Tax default properties can often be acquired for the owed back taxes, which can be significantly lower than the property's market value, offering the potential for high returns on investment.
- **Lower Competition:** Compared to traditional real estate markets, tax default investing may have less competition, as it requires specialized knowledge and due diligence.
- **Direct Ownership:** In tax deed sales, investors can gain full ownership of a property, allowing for a wide range of investment strategies, including rental, resale, or development.
- **Secured Investment:** With tax lien certificates, your investment is secured by the property itself, and you can earn a fixed rate of return or eventually acquire the property if the lien is not redeemed.

Cons:

- **Complexity and Risk:** Navigating tax laws and understanding the auction process can be complex. There's also the risk of purchasing properties with hidden problems, like structural issues or title disputes.
- **Capital Requirement:** While the initial investment might be lower than purchasing a property outright, investors need to have ready capital to pay for the tax liens or deeds at auction.
- **Management and Rehabilitation:** Acquired properties may require significant management effort or rehabilitation before they can be sold or rented, adding to the investment cost.
- **Regulatory Variability:** Laws and procedures for tax default investing vary significantly by jurisdiction, requiring investors to be knowledgeable about local regulations.

Resources for Learning More:

- **Educational Websites:** Platforms like TaxSaleLists.com and TaxLienUniversity.com offer courses, webinars, and guides on tax default investing, providing insights into the process, risks, and strategies.
- **Books:** Books such as "The 16% Solution" by Joel S. Moskowitz offer a comprehensive look into tax lien investing, including strategies for earning high returns.
- **Local Government Resources:** Many county and municipal websites provide information on their tax default auction processes, upcoming sales, and lists of available properties.
- **Workshops and Seminars:** Attending workshops and seminars focused on tax default investing can provide valuable insights from experienced investors and opportunities to network.

- **Real Estate Investment Groups:** Joining local or online real estate investment groups can connect you with other tax default investors, offering a platform for sharing experiences, advice, and opportunities.

Tax default investing presents a unique opportunity to acquire real estate at below-market prices, but it requires a solid understanding of the process, risks, and local regulations. By leveraging the available educational resources and connecting with a community of experienced investors, you can navigate the complexities of tax default investing and potentially unlock significant returns on your investment.

Wholetail

Wholetail investing combines elements of wholesale and retail real estate strategies. Investors purchase properties at a discount, often with minimal to no renovations, and then sell them to retail buyers at a markup, but below full market value. This approach seeks to balance the quick turnaround of wholesaling with the higher profit margins of retailing, without requiring extensive property improvements. Here are the advantages and disadvantages of wholetail investing, along with resources for further education.

Pros:

- **Lower Capital Requirement:** Compared to traditional fix-and-flip, wholetail investing typically requires less capital since it minimizes the need for extensive renovations.
- **Faster Turnaround:** By selling properties with minimal improvements, investors can often realize their profits quicker than traditional retailing, making it an attractive option for those looking to

generate cash flow rapidly.

- **Wider Buyer Pool:** Wholetail properties can appeal to a broader audience, including retail buyers looking for lower-priced homes they can customize and investors searching for deals with potential.
- **Reduced Risk:** With minimal investment in renovations, the risk of overcapitalizing on a property is lower, protecting profit margins.

Cons:

- **Market Sensitivity:** The success of wholetail investments can be highly sensitive to market conditions. In a slow market, the reduced margin may not cover holding and selling costs.
- **Limited Value Add:** Since the investment in improvements is minimal, there's less opportunity to significantly increase a property's value, which can cap potential profits.
- **Regulatory and Ethical Considerations:** Investors need to navigate disclosure requirements carefully and ethically, ensuring buyers are aware of the property's condition.
- **Competition:** In hot markets, finding discounted properties suitable for wholetailing can be competitive, requiring extensive marketing or network connections to source deals.

Resources for Learning More:

- **Real Estate Investment Associations (REIAs):** Joining a local REIA can provide access to seminars and workshops focusing on various investment strategies, including wholetailing.
- **Online Courses:** Platforms like Udemy and BiggerPockets offer courses taught by experienced real estate professionals that cover wholetail strategies, sourcing deals, and navigating the selling process.

- **Books:** While specific books on wholetailing are rare, many real estate investment books cover the principles that underpin wholetail strategies. Look for titles that focus on creative real estate solutions and hybrid investment strategies.
- **Podcasts and Blogs:** Listening to real estate investment podcasts and reading blogs can provide up-to-date insights on wholetailing. Experienced investors often share their strategies, successes, and lessons learned.
- **Networking Events:** Real estate networking events are invaluable for meeting other investors, potential buyers, and industry professionals who can offer advice, partnerships, and opportunities tailored to wholetail investing.

Wholetail investing offers an appealing balance between the quick flips of wholesaling and the profit potential of traditional retailing. However, its success depends on an investor's ability to find the right properties, understand market dynamics, and effectively market to potential buyers. By utilizing educational resources and building a strong network within the real estate community, investors can navigate the nuances of wholetail investing and capitalize on its unique advantages.

Creative Finance

Creative finance in real estate investing refers to non-traditional financing methods that go beyond conventional bank loans or cash transactions. These strategies can include lease options, seller financing, subject-to transactions, and more, offering flexible solutions for acquiring properties. Creative finance techniques can open doors for investors who might not have access to large amounts of capital or who seek to leverage their investments in innovative ways. Below are the pros and cons of creative finance investing, along with resources for further learning.

Pros:

- **Access to More Deals:** Creative financing allows investors to pursue deals that might not be feasible with traditional financing, broadening the scope of potential investments.
- **Less Capital Outlay:** Many creative finance strategies require less upfront capital than conventional purchases, enabling investors to retain cash for other investments or expenses.
- **Flexibility:** These methods offer flexible terms that can be customized to suit the needs of both the buyer and seller, often resulting in win-win scenarios.
- **Investing Leverage:** Creative finance can provide significant leverage, allowing investors to control properties and generate returns with minimal investment.

Cons:

- **Complexity and Risk:** Creative financing structures can be complex and carry unique risks, including legal and financial implications if not properly structured and executed.
- **Dependence on Seller Cooperation:** Many creative financing strategies rely on finding willing sellers who understand and agree to non-traditional terms, which can limit available opportunities.
- **Potential for Negative Cash Flow:** If not carefully planned, some creative finance deals, especially those with higher carrying costs or lower rental income, can result in negative cash flow.
- **Regulatory Challenges:** Navigating the legal and tax implications of creative finance deals requires thorough understanding and compliance to avoid potential issues.

Resources for Learning More:

- **Books:** Titles such as "Investing in Real Estate with Lease Options and Subject-To Deals" by Wendy Patton offer insights into specific creative financing strategies.
- **Online Platforms:** BiggerPockets and REIClub feature forums, articles, and webinars dedicated to creative real estate financing, where seasoned investors share their experiences and advice.
- **Educational Courses:** Platforms like Udemy offer courses on real estate creative financing, covering everything from basic principles to advanced strategies.
- **Networking Groups:** Local and online real estate investment groups often host discussions and workshops on creative financing, providing opportunities to learn from experienced investors and connect with potential partners.
- **Mentorship and Coaching:** Finding a mentor or coach who specializes in creative financing can provide personalized guidance and help navigate the complexities of these strategies.

Creative finance investing presents a viable alternative to traditional real estate financing, offering flexibility and access to deals that might otherwise be out of reach. However, its success depends on an investor's ability to understand and navigate the intricacies of each strategy. By leveraging educational resources and engaging with the real estate community, investors can develop the knowledge and skills necessary to effectively utilize creative finance in their investment endeavors.

Note Investing

Note investing involves the purchase and management of the debt secured by real estate, rather than the real estate itself. Investors buy mortgage notes or trust deeds, becoming the lender and receiving the mortgage payments from borrowers. This strategy can offer a unique blend of income generation and investment security, appealing to those interested in the financial side of real estate without the complexities of property management. Below are the advantages and disadvantages of note investing, along with resources for further education.

Pros:

- **Passive Income:** Note investing provides a stream of passive income through the receipt of regular mortgage payments, appealing to investors seeking less hands-on involvement.
- **Collateral Security:** The investment is secured by real estate, offering a tangible asset as collateral and reducing the risk of loss compared to unsecured investments.
- **Diversification:** Adding real estate notes to an investment portfolio can diversify risks, especially for those looking to balance out more volatile investments.
- **Flexibility:** Investors have the flexibility to buy, sell, or trade notes, allowing for various strategies and levels of involvement.

Cons:

- **Due Diligence Required:** Investors must conduct thorough due diligence on the borrower's creditworthiness and the property's value to mitigate risk, which can be time-consuming and requires expertise.

- **Default Risk:** There is a risk that borrowers may default on their payments, requiring investors to manage the foreclosure process, which can be lengthy and costly.
- **Market Knowledge:** Successful note investing requires an understanding of both the real estate market and the financial markets to assess the value and risk of notes accurately.
- **Liquidity:** Notes can be less liquid than other types of investments, potentially making it challenging to sell quickly without a discount.

Resources for Learning More:

- **Books:** "The Little Green Book of Note Investing" by Fred Moskowitz provides a comprehensive guide to the basics of note investing, strategies, and risk management.
- **Online Platforms:** Websites like NoteMBA and Paperstac offer platforms for learning about note investing, networking with other investors, and buying or selling notes.
- **Courses and Webinars:** Many online educational resources, including BiggerPockets and Udemy, offer courses specifically focused on note investing, covering everything from beginner basics to advanced strategies.
- **Real Estate Investment Groups:** Joining investment groups or forums that focus on note investing can be invaluable for networking, sharing experiences, and finding opportunities.
- **Conferences and Seminars:** Annual conferences and seminars on note investing provide opportunities to learn from experts, discover new trends, and connect with service providers.

Note investing offers an alternative path to real estate investment that focuses on financial instruments rather than physical properties. While it presents an opportunity for passive income and investment diversification, success in note investing requires careful due diligence, an understanding of market dynamics, and readiness to manage the risks associated with borrower defaults. By leveraging available educational resources and engaging with the note investing community, investors can gain the knowledge and connections needed to navigate this complex but potentially rewarding investment landscape.

Closing Thoughts:

In navigating the realm of real estate investing, identifying your North Star—your primary investment strategy—is crucial. It's about choosing a strategy that aligns with your personal and financial goals, whether that's through fix and flip, buy and hold, short-term rentals, tax default investing, wholetail, creative finance, or note investing. Each strategy offers unique challenges and rewards, but the right choice for you is the one that resonates with your aspirations and values.

5

Multiply Your Productivity

I n the fast-paced world of real estate investing, maximizing productivity is not just about working harder, but smarter. One of the most effective ways to enhance your efficiency and expand your capabilities is through strategic partnerships and outsourcing. By finding a business partner with complementary skills and outsourcing non-core functions to virtual assistants, you can significantly increase your operational capacity, allowing you to focus on high-value activities that directly contribute to your investment success.

Find a Business Partner

Securing a business partner with a complementary skill set is a strategic move that can significantly enhance the scope and success of your real estate investment endeavors. This partnership allows both parties to concentrate on their strengths, ensuring a more comprehensive approach to business challenges and opportunities. Here are the key benefits of finding such a partner:

- **Enhanced Expertise:** A partner with different skills can fill gaps in your own expertise, ensuring that all aspects of the business are managed with proficiency. For example, if you excel in financial analysis but lack marketing acumen, a partner who thrives in marketing and client relations can cover this crucial area.

- **Increased Efficiency:** By dividing responsibilities according to each partner's strengths, you can both work more efficiently, avoiding the learning curve and mistakes that come from venturing into unfamiliar territory.

- **Broader Network:** Each partner brings their own network of contacts, providing access to a wider pool of potential deals, investors, and industry professionals. This expanded network can open doors to opportunities that might otherwise be inaccessible.

- **Risk Sharing:** Real estate investments come with inherent risks. Having a partner means you can share both the financial burden and the decision-making, mitigating individual risk and stress.

- **Support and Motivation:** Real estate investing can be a demanding and sometimes isolating venture. A partner offers moral support, helping to maintain motivation and resilience through challenges.

- **Innovative Problem Solving:** Different perspectives can foster innovative solutions to business challenges. A partner can offer alternative viewpoints and strategies, enriching the decision-making process.

Finding the right business partner involves identifying someone whose skills complement your own and whose investment goals and values align with yours. Networking events, real estate investment groups, and online platforms are excellent places to start your search. It's crucial to thoroughly vet potential partners, considering not just their professional capabilities but also their reliability and compatibility with your business philosophy.

Outsource

Outsourcing non-core activities such as inbound lead capture, direct mail marketing, cold calling, and administrative tasks is a strategic approach that allows real estate investors to focus on income-producing activities. Here's how outsourcing these functions can benefit your business:

- **Focus on Core Activities:** Delegating routine or specialized tasks to external providers frees up your time and energy to concentrate on strategic investment decisions and growth opportunities.
- **Cost Efficiency:** Outsourcing can be more cost-effective than hiring full-time employees, especially for tasks that don't require a permanent staff member. You can scale up or down based on current business needs without the overhead of salaries and benefits.
- **Access to Expertise:** Service providers specializing in real estate-related tasks bring expertise and efficiency to their work, often delivering better results than if these tasks were handled in-house without the same level of skill.
- **Increased Flexibility:** With responsibilities like lead generation and administrative duties in the hands of competent external teams, you can quickly adapt to market changes and business demands without the need to manage additional staff.
- **Enhanced Productivity:** Outsourcing allows you to operate more efficiently, ensuring that every aspect of your business is managed by someone who is fully focused on that area. This leads to faster turnaround times, higher quality output, and ultimately, better results for your investment activities.

To start outsourcing effectively, identify the specific tasks that are essential yet time-consuming and find reputable service providers who specialize in those areas. Platforms like Upwork, Fiverr, or specialized real estate virtual assistant companies can be excellent resources for finding skilled professionals. Clear communication of your expectations and ongoing management of these relationships are key to maximizing the benefits of outsourcing for your real estate investment business.

Closing Thoughts:

By strategically partnering and outsourcing, you can not only multiply your productivity but also enhance your investment business's growth potential and resilience. This approach allows you to focus on what you do best, leveraging others' strengths to cover more ground and achieve your investment goals more efficiently.

6

Accountability

In the realm of real estate investing, accountability is the compass that keeps you oriented towards your goals, ensuring that every step taken is a step forward. The adage "Failing to plan is planning to fail" rings especially true here. Establishing a routine of daily and weekly meetings to monitor progress, discuss activities, and review key performance indicators (KPIs) can significantly enhance your project's success rate. This chapter outlines strategies for integrating accountability into your investment activities, enabling you to stay on course and make necessary adjustments for optimal performance.

Daily Stand-Ups

Implementing daily stand-ups is a powerful practice in real estate investing that involves brief, focused conversations about the day's planned activities. These meetings serve as a platform for team members to share updates on their progress, outline their goals for the day, and discuss any potential roadblocks that could impede their work.

Benefits:

- **Enhanced Communication:** Daily stand-ups foster open communication among team members, ensuring everyone is aware of what others are working on and how it affects their tasks.
- **Increased Efficiency:** By setting clear objectives for the day, team members can work more efficiently towards their goals, knowing exactly what needs to be accomplished.
- **Early Identification of Roadblocks:** Discussing potential challenges at the outset allows the team to identify and address roadblocks early, preventing delays and maintaining project momentum.
- **Accountability:** Regular check-ins promote a sense of accountability, as team members are expected to report on their progress and deliver on their commitments each day.
- **Team Cohesion:** Daily stand-ups strengthen team cohesion by encouraging collaboration and mutual support, as members can offer assistance to colleagues facing challenges.

Implementation:

To make daily stand-ups effective, keep them concise and focused. Conduct these meetings at the same time each day to establish a routine, and limit them to 15 minutes to ensure they are time-efficient. If working with a remote team, utilize video conferencing tools to maintain a personal connection and foster team unity.

In summary, daily stand-ups are a cornerstone of a productive real estate investment team, enabling swift communication, promoting efficiency, and facilitating the early resolution of issues. This practice ensures that every team member starts their day with a clear understanding of their objectives and the support they need to overcome any obstacles.

Weekly Performance Reviews

Weekly performance reviews in real estate investing are strategic sessions aimed at analyzing the week's outcomes, identifying trends in deal flow, and pinpointing high-level issues that require attention. These meetings are crucial for evaluating the effectiveness of your investment strategies and ensuring alignment with your long-term goals.

Benefits:

- **Trend Identification:** Regular reviews allow you to spot trends and patterns in deal flow, enabling quick identification of successful strategies or areas needing improvement.
- **Strategic Insight:** Analyzing weekly performance provides valuable insights into the overall health of your investment portfolio, highlighting opportunities for growth and areas of risk.
- **Problem Detection:** By reviewing key performance indicators (KPIs) and deal flow, you can quickly detect issues affecting your investment activities, allowing for timely intervention.
- **Goal Alignment:** These meetings ensure that all team members are aligned with the investment goals and understand how their work contributes to achieving these objectives.
- **Motivation and Engagement:** Discussing weekly achievements and challenges keeps the team motivated and engaged, fostering a culture of continuous improvement and collective success.

Implementation:

Conduct weekly performance reviews with a structured agenda, focusing on KPIs, deal flow analysis, and strategic discussions. Encourage open dialogue, allowing team members to share their insights and suggestions for improvement. Utilize data visualization tools to present information clearly and facilitate easier understanding of trends and performance metrics.

In essence, weekly performance reviews are instrumental in maintaining the strategic direction of your real estate investment activities. They provide a regular checkpoint for assessing progress, adjusting strategies, and reinforcing team alignment towards shared goals.

Course Correction

The ability to quickly make adjustments in response to performance reviews or unexpected challenges is crucial in real estate investing. Course correction involves modifying strategies, reallocating resources, or changing tactics to address underperformance or capitalize on new opportunities.

Benefits:

- **Agility:** Quick adjustments ensure your investment strategy remains responsive to market changes and internal performance metrics, maintaining your competitive edge.
- **Risk Mitigation:** Timely corrections help mitigate risks associated with underperforming assets or strategies, reducing potential losses and protecting your investment.
- **Opportunistic Investing:** Being able to pivot quickly allows you to take advantage of emerging opportunities, whether they arise from market trends or unforeseen circumstances.
- **Efficiency:** Course corrections streamline operations by eliminating ineffective practices and focusing resources on the most productive

areas.

Implementation:

Implement a system for monitoring performance indicators and market conditions that can trigger a review of current strategies. Establish clear protocols for decision-making and executing changes, ensuring that all team members understand how and when adjustments will be made. Encourage a culture of adaptability, where feedback is welcomed and changes are implemented swiftly to capitalize on insights gained from performance reviews.

Course correction is a dynamic aspect of real estate investing, allowing you to adapt and refine your approach continually. By staying flexible and responsive, you can navigate the complexities of the market and steer your investment activities toward sustained success.

Avoid Shiny Object Syndrome

Avoiding shiny object syndrome is crucial for maintaining strategic focus in real estate investing. This syndrome represents the temptation to chase new, exciting opportunities that deviate from your core strategy, potentially diverting resources and attention away from your primary goals.

Staying Focused:

- **Recognize Distractions:** Develop an awareness of when an opportunity is truly aligned with your strategy versus when it's merely a distraction. This discernment is key to maintaining focus.
- **Reaffirm Goals:** Regularly revisit and reaffirm your investment

goals and strategies. This practice helps anchor your decisions and keeps your efforts directed toward your long-term objectives.

- **Strategic Evaluation:** Before pursuing any new opportunity, evaluate it against your established goals and criteria. Ask whether it brings you closer to your objectives or pulls you away from them.
- **Accountability Measures:** Implement accountability mechanisms, such as regular check-ins with a mentor or business partner, to ensure that your actions remain aligned with your strategic plan.

Benefits:

- **Resource Optimization:** By staying focused, you optimize the use of your most valuable resources—time, capital, and energy—ensuring they are invested in activities that directly contribute to your goals.
- **Increased Productivity:** Eliminating distractions allows for more efficient progress toward your objectives, enhancing overall productivity and effectiveness.
- **Strategic Consistency:** Maintaining a clear, consistent strategy facilitates better decision-making and more predictable outcomes, building a solid foundation for long-term success.

In essence, avoiding shiny object syndrome is about disciplined adherence to your strategic vision. It requires vigilant self-awareness and commitment to your goals, ensuring that every effort is purposefully aligned with your desired outcomes. This focused approach is instrumental in navigating the complexities of real estate investing and achieving sustained success.

Closing Thoughts:

By embedding accountability into the fabric of your investment operations, you establish a structured approach to achieving success. Daily stand-ups and weekly performance reviews are not just meetings; they are the pillars upon which a disciplined, results-driven investment strategy is built.

7

Winning

I n the competitive landscape of real estate investing, recognizing and celebrating all wins, big and small, is crucial for maintaining momentum and morale. Equally important is the discipline to stay focused on your established strategy, resisting the allure of new opportunities that don't align with your long-term goals. This chapter delves into the importance of acknowledging achievements and the strategies to avoid the pitfalls of shiny object syndrome, ensuring a focused and successful investment journey.

Celebrate All Wins

Celebrating all wins, both large and small, plays a pivotal role in the journey of real estate investing. This practice not only acknowledges the hard work and dedication required to achieve these milestones but also has a profound compounding effect on the business's morale, culture, and performance.

Benefits:

- **Motivation Boost:** Recognizing achievements energizes the team, fueling motivation and enthusiasm for tackling future challenges. This positive reinforcement encourages continuous effort and dedication.
- **Team Cohesion:** Celebrations bring team members together, fostering a sense of unity and shared purpose. This enhanced team cohesion strengthens collaboration and supports a healthy, productive work environment.
- **Reinforcement of Successful Behaviors:** Acknowledging specific actions that led to success reinforces those behaviors, encouraging their repetition in future endeavors. This learning mechanism helps refine strategies and processes over time.
- **Psychological Well-being:** Celebrations contribute to overall well-being by providing moments of joy and satisfaction. They remind individuals of their value to the organization and the tangible impact of their contributions.
- **Compounding Effect:** The practice of celebrating wins creates a positive feedback loop. Success breeds success, as each achievement builds confidence and ambition, setting the stage for further accomplishments. This compounding effect accelerates progress and amplifies the overall impact on the business.

Implementation:

To effectively celebrate wins, establish a culture that values and recognizes contributions at all levels. This can be achieved through regular acknowledgment in team meetings, celebratory messages or emails, achievement awards, or team outings. The key is to match the celebration's scale to the significance of the win, ensuring that recognition feels genuine and meaningful.

In summary, celebrating all wins cultivates a positive, success-oriented environment that motivates individuals, enhances team dynamics, and solidifies the behaviors that drive achievement. This practice not only appreciates past successes but also propels the team toward future victories, embodying the principle that every win, no matter its size, is a step forward in the business's journey.

8

Conclusion

Embarking on the journey of real estate investing while managing the demands of a full-time job is no small feat. It requires dedication, strategic planning, and a commitment to continuous learning and adaptation. Throughout this book, we've explored the foundational steps and strategies necessary to build a thriving real estate business, emphasizing the importance of establishing relationships, diving into the real estate circle, aligning with your North Star, multiplying your productivity, maintaining accountability, and celebrating every win, all while staying focused on your established strategy.

The path to successful real estate investing is as diverse as the investors who walk it. Whether you're drawn to the quick turns of fix-and-flip, the long-term growth of buy-and-hold, the innovative approaches of creative financing, or the passive income potential of note investing, the key to success lies in leveraging your unique strengths and resources. By finding a business partner with complementary skills, outsourcing non-core tasks, and embracing the power of accountability and productivity tools, you can significantly enhance your ability to manage and grow your investment portfolio alongside your career.

Celebrating wins, both big and small, fosters a culture of positivity and achievement, driving motivation and team cohesion. Simultaneously, avoiding the pitfalls of shiny object syndrome by maintaining a laser focus on your strategic goals ensures that your efforts are both efficient and effective. Remember, real estate investing is not just about acquiring assets; it's about building a sustainable business that can provide financial freedom, security, and a legacy.

As you move forward, keep in mind that the world of real estate is dynamic and ever-evolving. Market conditions change, new opportunities arise, and challenges emerge. Staying informed, flexible, and responsive to these changes is crucial. Continue to educate yourself, engage with your network, and leverage the collective wisdom and experiences of the real estate community. The strategies and principles outlined in this book are not static; they're meant to be adapted and refined as you grow and learn.

In closing, the journey of real estate investing is both challenging and rewarding. It demands hard work, perseverance, and a strategic mindset, but the rewards—financial independence, personal growth, and the satisfaction of building something of lasting value—are immeasurable. As you embark on or continue this journey, remember that every step forward is a step towards realizing your vision of success in real estate investing.

Let this book be your guide, but also your starting point. The real lessons come from the experiences you'll gather, the relationships you'll build, and the challenges you'll overcome. Embrace the journey with enthusiasm, resilience, and an unwavering commitment to your goals.

The world of real estate investing is vast and full of potential; with the right approach, it's yours to explore and conquer.

If you found this book helpful, I would be very appreciative if you left a favorable review for the book on Amazon!

9

Resources

C hatGPT. GPT-4, OpenAI, 2024, https://www.openai.com.

Michelli, Joseph A. *The Airbnb Way: 5 Leadership Lessons for Igniting Growth through Loyalty, Community, and Belonging.* McGraw-Hill, 2020.

Moskowitz, Fred. *The Little Green Book Of Note Investing: A Practical Guide for Getting Started with Investing in Mortgage Notes.* Take Note Publishing, LLC, 2020.

Moskowitz, Joel S. *The 16% Solution: How to Get High Interest Rates in a Low-Interest World with Tax Lien Certificates.* 2nd ed. revised and Updated, Andrews McMeel Pub, 2009.

Patton, Wendy. *Investing in Real Estate with Lease Options and "Subject-to" Deals: Powerful Strategies for Getting More When You Sell, and Paying Less When You Buy.* Second edition., W. Patton, 2023.

Ribbers, Jasper, and Eric D. Moller. *Get Paid for Your Pad.* https://getpaidforyourpad.com/podcast-2/.

Scott, J. *The Book on Flipping Houses: How to Buy, Rehab, and Resell Residential Properties.* Revised edition, BiggerPockets Publishing, 2019.

Turner, Brandon. *The Book on Rental Property Investing: How to Create Wealth and Passive Income through Smart Buy & Hold Real Estate Investing.*

Revised edition, BiggerPockets, 2016.